introducing the

Friends of the Western Buddhist Order

Published by
Windhorse Publications,
11 Park Road, Birmingham B13 8AB

©Vishvapani 2001

The right of Vishvapani to be identified as the author of this work has been
asserted by him in accordance with the Copyright, Designs and Patents Act 1988

Design
Vincent Stokes

Printed by
Interprint Ltd, Marsa, Malta

British Library Cataloguing in Publication Data:
A catalogue record for this book is available from the British Library
ISBN 0 904766 98 5

introducing the

Friends of the Western Buddhist Order

Vishvapani

Windhorse Publications

contents

3

preface

A plainly-clad Japanese meditator sits before a wall, patiently waiting for his mind to become quiet. A yellow-robed monk paces back and forth, his movements filled with awareness, every step a meditation. A Tibetan lama intones a deep-throated chant, candlelight flecking his maroon robes and the many-headed Buddhas on the shrine. A statue of a Buddha rests amid the ruins of an ancient temple in the Cambodian jungle, its face lit by a smile of kindness and understanding.

These are images of Buddhism as it has existed in Asia, and similar images are now to be seen in Western countries as well. Over the two-and-a-half millennia of the history of Buddhism people from many Asian cultures have applied the Buddha's teachings to their lives. As the centuries rolled by, new forms of practice developed, and new expressions of the Buddha's timeless insights were found to suit the changing circumstances. But how can the Buddha's message be expressed in the today's world?

A woman rises for morning meditation in the residential community where she lives with Buddhist friends in the heart of London. An artist wrestles with his latest Buddha statue, combining classical Greek forms with traditional Asian ones. A worker in a Right Livelihood business sits before his computer screen. A parent gets up from meditation to meet the demands of child-care and family life with patience and compassion. An Indian Buddhist teaches meditation to hundreds of people in the crowded corridor of a Bombay slum. A man sits in deep meditation in a remote Spanish valley, living a simple life of renunciation, but dressed in Western clothes.

These are images of people who follow the Buddha's teachings within the Friends of the Western Buddhist Order (FWBO): a modern Buddhist movement that applies the universal insights of the Buddha in the new conditions of the modern world. The FWBO has eighty centres around the world, and activities in twenty-five countries. It is a dynamic spiritual community of men and women who together follow the Buddha's path.

This book is a short introduction to the FWBO explaining its principles, its relationship to the Buddhist tradition as a whole, and its practice.

5

introduction: the way of the Buddha

The Buddha's message

The word `Buddha' is a title, not a name. It means `one who is awake', so a Buddha is someone who in a profound and mysterious sense has woken up from the slumber of the human condition. It was first given to a man who was born Siddhartha Gautama, in Nepal, 2,500 years ago, and the Buddhist tradition starts with his Awakening.

Many people in the West have been attracted to Buddhism because of the power of the Buddha's story. As a young man, Siddhartha led the privileged life of a prince, surrounded by all the luxuries and pleasures he could desire and protected from harsh realities. But when he encountered an old man, a sick man, and a corpse, Siddhartha experienced deep disillusionment with his life, seeing that it did not confront suffering and impermanence. He left home for the forest, following a tradition of renunciation and spiritual endeavour that was already a long-established part of Indian culture.

After many trials Siddhartha sat down to meditate with an unshakeable determination that `flesh may wither and blood dry up, but I will not move from this spot until Enlightenment has been reached by me.' The image of Siddhartha beneath the bodhi tree, poised in utmost stillness, has been depicted many times in Buddhist art, and has stirred the imagination of Westerners. It is an image of a solitary human being *paying attention to*

reality. Through many years of meditation Siddhartha's mind had become free of distractions, and his heart was purified of greed, selfishness, and hatred. As the morning star rose in the east, the legend says, a transformative understanding arose in Siddhartha. He became the Buddha, the Awakened One.

Everything that follows in this book springs from Siddhartha's Awakening. The Buddha's teachings, which he called the Dharma, were `wake-up calls', attempts to communicate this experience so that others could share in it. The Buddhist tradition has grown up from the efforts of many generations to respond to these calls, and the FWBO is one such response.

Some of the concepts in which the Dharma has been formulated will be encountered later in this book, but the point of these teachings and their meaning for individuals has been powerfully expressed in metaphors. One such metaphor comes from the period immediately following the Buddha's Enlightenment. We are told that he wondered whether it would be possible for others to understand his experience. The answer came to him in a vision of humanity as a bed of lotus flowers. Some of the flowers were still submerged in the mud, others were just emerging from it, and others again

were on the point of blossoming. In other words, the Buddha saw that all beings have the potential for spiritual unfoldment and awakening, and that some need just a little help for this potential to be realized. Following this metaphor one could say that practising the Dharma means growing, like a bud coming into flower. It is a path of spiritual development.

Another metaphor sees the Dharma as a mirror that reveals the true nature of our experience, and suggests how to change it. When we look in the mirror we see that life contains an inescapable element of pain and unsatisfactoriness. Everything is impermanent, and although we shy away from this fact, the greatest certainty of our lives is that we will die. Life is shifting and ungraspable, despite our efforts to pin it down and find security. It is hard to bear very much reality, and we need to learn to contemplate these truths calmly and joyfully if we are to absorb them. It is up to us whether we want to look into the Buddha's mirror and act on what it reveals. According to this image, Buddhism is a way of seeing the truth.

A third Buddhist image is of a net of jewels – Indra's net – spread out through infinite space. Each jewel is so perfectly polished that it reflects all

the other jewels, reflects their reflections of each other, and is itself reflected in each. This is an image of the interconnectedness of all existence. The great illusion is that we are separate, and because we believe this illusion, we come to think we are the centre of life. Indra's net is an image of our deep involvement in the world. Practising the Dharma means living in accordance with this image – seeing others with kindness, and opening to life rather than trying to control it.

The key to realizing the truth lies within us. As a famous Buddhist text, the *Dhammapada*, says: `All things proceed from the mind.' Meditation is the most important way in which Buddhists understand and transform their minds, but the Buddha insisted that every moment is an opportunity to become more loving, generous, and aware. Practising the Dharma means learning to live in ways that are creative, engaged with others, and open to life's truths. It involves discipline and scrupulous self-examination, but perhaps most eloquently the Dharma is described as `liberation'. When asked what quality distinguished his teaching the Buddha replied: `Just as the ocean has one taste, the taste of salt, so my teaching has one taste, the taste of freedom' (*The Udana*).

Head of Buddha figure at the Manchester Buddhist Centre photograph by Devamitra

Shakyamuni Buddha

photograph by Vincent Stokes

Buddhism in history

How have these principles worked out in practice? As a cultural phenomenon Buddhism began when the Buddha started to teach. In the forty-five years between the Buddha's Enlightenment and his death, he travelled throughout northern India, communicating with the people he met. We have records of his conversations with priests, robbers, kings, farmers, prostitutes, lunatics, and sages. Many decided to follow the Buddha's teachings, and often these disciples gained Enlightenment themselves. They passed on what they learned to others, and in this way an unbroken chain of teaching and realization has continued down to the present day.

Over the next 2,500 years Buddhism spread across Asia to be practised by Tibetan nomads and Chinese aristocrats, Indian scholars and Japanese poets. But what is the legacy that remains today? Many schools of Buddhism developed, and we can still see their art, read their texts, and, in some cases, meet their living representatives. Sometimes these schools were expressions of the fresh insights into the Dharma by a great teacher. Sometimes they were adaptations of previous schools that had arrived in new cultures. Sometimes they were reform movements instigated by people who felt that the spirit of the teaching had been buried beneath religious institutions, or that practices had degenerated into formalism. What is clear is that there is no single form that alone is the true expression of the Dharma. It has had to be rediscovered and re-expressed in every generation according to the conditions that prevail.

Some of the Buddhist schools survive in the modern world as vibrant spiritual communities and lineages of practice; others have died out altogether; others again have preserved an ossified form of Buddhist practice that had its heyday hundreds or even thousands of years ago. These schools often developed in isolation from one another, sometimes in ignorance of one another's teachings. Each expresses its values and its perspective on the path to Enlightenment in its own vocabulary, and these vocabularies often owe much to the national culture in which they developed. And developments in Buddhist doctrines have led to disagreement about what authentic Buddhist teaching should include.

In the last century or so, Buddhism has faced challenges as great as any in its history in the encounter with what, as shorthand, we can call modernity – the complex, secularized, and technologically powered cultures and societies that have replaced traditional social structures across much of the world. The most pressing question is whether it can survive at all. Scholars estimate that a hundred years ago a third of the world's population lived in countries that were strongly influenced by Buddhism. But Buddhism was persecuted in countries that became communist, and elsewhere it has lost much of its traditional role as cultures have been transformed by technology and consumer capitalism, or targeted by Christian missionaries.

A second challenge arises from the encounter between Buddhist traditions, and the light thrown on this meeting by historical scholarship. Buddhists are being forced to ask if Buddhism is one or many; if the differences between the schools are more important than what they have in common; if it is possible to distinguish the Dharma – the teachings in principle – from the cultural forms in which they have been expressed; and if some of these teachings need to be revised in the light of science and history. Buddhists are being forced to dig deep into their tradition to address these crises.

Crossing cultures

Since the nineteenth century growing numbers of people from non-Buddhist countries have looked to Buddhism as a source of wisdom and inspiration (not only in the West, but in India as well, for example). Early in the twentieth century a trickle of Westerners took up Dharma practice, sometimes travelling to Asia to study. In the 1960s the trickle became a flood. Many of those who went abroad have returned to the West where they have shared what they learned, and been joined by Asian teachers.

In countries that have been shaped by modernity, Buddhism has encountered a deep need for spiritual guidance, and for a credible and effective spiritual path. Many Westerners see Buddhism as a source of insights that are uncannily relevant to modern culture, and as a repository of practices for surviving it. The Dalai Lama has become a popular icon; meditation is known as a resource for overcoming stress and cultivating an inner life of self-awareness; artists and thinkers in many fields have been influenced by Buddhist ideas. And there are now many practitioners of Zen, Theravada, Vajrayana, and other Buddhist traditions in Western countries. In North America up to 1,000,000 people have become Buddhists, and in the UK the figure is 40–50,000.

But even though Buddhism has become popular in the West, crucial issues remain. When Buddhism first travelled to China it was several centuries before a recognizably indigenous Chinese Buddhism emerged. For Buddhism to be successfully translated from an Asian tradition to something that is a natural idiom for the spiritual lives of Westerners, important issues need to be addressed.

The first issue is that of distinguishing the universal principles of the Dharma from their expression in Asian cultural forms. Many Buddhists in the West have chosen to follow one or other of the traditions that have been transplanted from Asia. For such people the challenge is to discover which elements are relevant to them and which are expressions of an Asian culture. Tibetan dress or Japanese etiquette are not in themselves intrinsic to the path to Awakening – wearing a robe does not in itself make you any wiser. More difficult still, the teachings of particular traditions can express a cast of mind that is also culturally conditioned, and may therefore be alien to outsiders. For example, in many Asian cultures the doctrine of rebirth is accepted without question, but it will be seen very differently by sceptical, rationalist Westerners. More broadly, many traditions have had little awareness of the historical circumstances within which their scriptures, doctrines, and practices developed, and their self-understandings are often at variance with what modern scholarship tells us.

This is not to suggest that Zen, Theravada, Vajrayana, and so on cannot be effective means of spiritual development for modern people. But, as many Western practitioners of Asian Buddhist traditions have come to acknowledge, all forms of Buddhism face crucial issues of cultural translation in the transition from traditional societies to modernity, and from Asia to the West.

For those who do not follow a single tradition, an alternative approach is eclecticism. Faced by the bewildering variety of Buddhist texts, teachers, and meditation techniques now available in the West, one response is to pick and choose those bits that seem attractive, and perhaps – in the manner of the New Age – to add elements of other spiritual traditions. But the danger in this approach is that one's engagement will remain sporadic and superficial, and avoid teachings that are challenging and difficult, and that require patient effort to change oneself.

In a similar vein we can try to adapt the Dharma to fit our values, but in doing so we risk distorting it in through the lens of our own (often unconscious) views and assumptions. The Dharma has a coherent view of life, and teaches values that derive from that view. These have the potential to challenge or even to transform Western values. So on the one hand Westerners cannot adopt an Asian world-view while maintaining their intellectual, cultural, and spiritual integrity. On the other hand, if they simply judge Buddhism by Western standards, taking only those elements that fit easily, its message will be lost.

But despite these difficulties there is something universal in the Buddha's message that can cross the centuries, jump cultures, and speak directly to us. This is acknowledged by many followers of the Asian Buddhist traditions, especially when they consider what they have in common with other Buddhists, and it is the starting point for the FWBO. It neither wants to bring traditional Asian culture to the West, nor to make Buddhism fit Western predilections. Steering a middle path between identifying with one Asian tradition and eclectically drawing on all of them, the FWBO identifies the core that underlies all the Buddhist traditions and bases its own teachings on this.

Then it makes cultural connections, and explores questions of lifestyle so that we can put these core Buddhist teachings into practice in our own lives.

The FWBO has not definitively solved the question of what Buddhism should look like in the modern world, and it is not alone in its efforts to do so. But the story of its development, the thinking on which it is based, the lives of its members, the practices it teaches, the effect it is having on the world, and the structures it has developed, are important contributions in bringing the Dharma alive today.

Panos Pictures

13

a Buddhist movement for
the modern world

Sangharakshita

The story of the FWBO starts with its founder, a remarkable Englishman named Sangharakshita, who deserves to be seen as one of the founding fathers of Western Buddhism. Sangharakshita was born Dennis Lingwood in South London in 1925, and grew up in a very ordinary working-class family, but he was a prodigiously intelligent child who read voraciously and developed an interest in the cultures and philosophies of the East. At sixteen he read the *Diamond Sutra* and realized he was a Buddhist. Thus he became involved in London's germinal Buddhist world in wartime Britain, and started to study and practise Buddhism intensively.

Conscription took him to the Far East, and after the war he stayed on in India. He was ordained as a Buddhist monk, and thereafter went by the name Sangharakshita ('he who is protected by the spiritual community'). Sangharakshita lived for many years in Kalimpong, in north-eastern India, where he studied with teachers from several of the major Buddhist traditions including leading Tibetan Buddhist lamas.

During this period Sangharakshita became well known for a non-sectarian approach that drew on the whole Buddhist tradition, especially through his book *A Survey of Buddhism*, and as editor of the *Maha Bodhi Journal*. He also helped in the revival of Buddhism in India, particularly through his participation in the movement of conversion to Buddhism of millions of people who were considered 'untouchables' under the Hindu social system. The new Buddhists were mostly very poor, and one thing Sangharakshita learned from working with them was that Buddhism must address people's social conditions as well as their minds.

Sangharakshita has always written a

**Urgyen
Sangharakshita**
photograph by
Moksajyoti,
© Clear Vision

great deal, and he is now the author of over forty books which have been translated into many languages. In these works he has addressed the major aspects of the Buddhist tradition, drawing inspiration from them in the light of traditional understandings, modern scholarship, and his own spiritual life. He is also a poet and the author of several volumes of memoirs, as well as works exploring aspects of Western culture and the arts from a Buddhist perspective.

The FWBO is based on Sangharakshita's approach to the Dharma. From the start of his career Sangharakshita has sought to understand what is at the heart of the Buddhist tradition and to re-express that in ways that are relevant, coherent, and spiritually vital. This has made him an innovative and creative figure in the Buddhist world who has provoked many responses and some controversy. Sangharakshita's later life has been devoted to bringing Buddhism to the modern world through his books and the movement he founded. But in the scope of his learning (as regards both Buddhist and Western thought) and the depth of his spiritual experience, Sangharakshita's life is itself an embodiment of the Dharma in a Western form.

Urgyen
Sangharakshita,
London, 1960s

The movement's development

Invited by members of Britain's small Buddhist community, Sangharakshita returned to England in the mid-1960s. He quickly saw that many people in Britain were open to Buddhism and might respond to its teachings. His own path had been one of exploration and experiment based on a deep commitment. Now that he was addressing Westerners he needed to discover forms of teaching and practice that would most effectively communicate the Buddha's teaching to the people he was meeting.

In 1967 Sangharakshita established the Friends of the Western Sangha, which changed its name a year later to the Friends of the Western Buddhist Order (FWBO). In 1968 he performed his first ordinations within the Western Buddhist Order (WBO), which was to be at the heart of the new movement.

Sangharakshita did not have a blueprint for what the movement would look like in the future, but he was clear about its principles. At the core was an Order, not a society or organization. Membership of the Order was determined not by payment of a membership fee, or by intellectual knowledge of Buddhism, but by commitment to the Buddha's path. The FWBO was the name of the activities, organizations, and community of Buddhists that developed around the Order. He intended the movement to grow naturally from the efforts of Order members to practise the Dharma under his guidance and share what they learned with others.

**Shrine at the
Buddhist Centre
in Essen**
photograph by
Devamitra

Sangharakshita started activities in a basement in London, and taught all the classes, gave all the lectures, and led every course and retreat. He soon attracted many people who responded to his approach, and the first centres opened in which Order members taught meditation and Buddhism. Following their experience of the more intensive and satisfying conditions on retreats, some people started living communally, and in this way the first residential communities developed. As people became more committed to their Dharma practice they also wanted to work together co-operatively. The businesses they established were seen as applications of the Buddha's teaching of Right Livelihood, and came to be known as `team-based Right Livelihood businesses'.

There are many other aspects to the movement, which are described in this book, and it might best be characterized as a germinal Buddhist culture. It has grown steadily, and at the time of writing, in mid-2000, there are around eighty centres, and activities in twenty-five countries. The UK is still the most important base for its work; but it has a significant presence in Australasia, and is increasingly well established in Western Europe and in North and South America. In 1978 several Order members moved to India to continue Sangharakshita's work among the new Buddhists, and there are now over twenty centres and 210 Order members in India. Worldwide the Order had grown into a spiritual community of nearly a thousand men and women.

Sangharakshita has handed over his responsibilities to a group of his senior Order members who are based at Madhyamaloka in Birmingham, England. The celebration of Sangharakshita's seventy-fifth birthday at Aston University in Birmingham on 26 August 2000 marked an important transition for the movement. Firstly, Sangharakshita handed on his responsibilities as Head of the Order to his senior disciples.

five ways of looking at the
Friends of the Western Buddhist Order

Since 1967 the FWBO has grown to be one of the leading Buddhist movements in the West, with centres and activities in many cities, and many more in India. To do justice to that variety this book will employ five ways of answering the question 'What is the FWBO?' It can be seen as:

An approach to Buddhism
A spiritual community
An engagement with society
A path of practice
A worldwide Buddhist movement

An approach to Buddhism

The FWBO is part of the Buddhist tradition, and its central teachings are those that are at the heart of the tradition as a whole. That is to say, it is devoted to following the Buddhist path. But the FWBO's relationship to the Buddhist tradition is governed by several founding principles: the central role of what is called `Going for Refuge to the Three Jewels' in the Buddhist spiritual life, concentrating on the fundamental Buddhist teachings, and drawing inspiration from the whole of the Buddhist tradition. Outward forms of the FWBO vary in the differing cultures where its members live, and they have developed over time, but these principles unify the movement and underlie its particular manifestations.

GOING FOR REFUGE TO THE THREE JEWELS

The purpose of all Buddhist schools is to teach a path to Enlightenment that will enable practitioners to become like the Buddha. What makes someone a Buddhist is their commitment to this endeavour, and all the doctrines, practices, institutions, and schools of Buddhism are useful to the extent that they help people to follow the Buddhist path. The traditional way in which Buddhists of all schools express this commitment is to say that they `go for Refuge to the Buddha, Dharma, and Sangha' (the Three Jewels).

Sangharakshita emphasizes that the Buddhist tradition is united by the defining act of Going for Refuge to the Three Jewels. This is the key to being a Buddhist, though some schools may well have lost sight of its full significance. Going for Refuge to the Three Jewels is the central principle or orientation of the FWBO, and all its activities are understood in relation to it.

The whole Buddhist tradition derives from the Buddha, and all Buddhist traditions regard him as their ultimate founder, guide, and inspiration. Going for Refuge to the Buddha means seeing the historical Buddha as one's ultimate teacher and spiritual guide. It also means committing oneself to achieving Buddhahood – Enlightenment for the sake of all beings – which is the goal of the Buddhist spiritual life. In other words, Going for Refuge to the Buddha means taking the Buddha as a guide and exemplar, deciding that he is one's personal spiritual ideal, and that one's life will be devoted to becoming Awakened like him.

`Dharma' means the teachings of the Buddha, the path to Enlightenment, and also the truth the Buddha himself realized. It is the content and expression of the Buddha's Enlightenment, as well as the means of reaching Enlightenment. So regarding the Dharma as a Refuge means seeing these teachings as the best guide to reality, and committing oneself to practising them.

If we are to practise the Dharma we need the example of others who have done so before us – especially those who have gained insight into reality themselves. These people are collectively known as the `Aryasangha', or spiritual community of the noble ones. More broadly, `sangha' also refers to the people with whom we share our spiritual lives. We need the guidance of personal teachers who are further along the path than we are, and the friendship of other practitioners.

The Three Jewels are not refuges in the sense that they enable us to avoid life's difficulties. The point is that worldly values cannot be relied on, but the ultimate aim of Going for Refuge to the Three Jewels is that one becomes the Three Jewels, one ultimately reaches Buddhahood, and one also realizes the Dharma and joins the Aryasangha. Then one is free from the fear and craving that are the causes of suffering. So Going for Refuge to the Three Jewels is not about believing in things that are external to oneself so much as orienting one's life in relation to ideals that go far beyond ordinary experience, and drawing one's values from them.

Sangharakshita emphasizes that Going for Refuge to the Three Jewels is the central and defining act of the Buddhist spiritual life. In a tradition that goes back to the Buddha, reciting the verses of Going for Refuge is the act by which one becomes a Buddhist, and every day around the world millions of Buddhists reassert their devotion to them.

Sangharakshita also emphasizes that Going for Refuge to the Three Jewels is not something one does once. It is how one orients one's life, not a single event or action. So one can say that the Buddhist spiritual life consists in Going for Refuge more and more deeply. Whatever stage one has reached, the task is always to take the next step in transforming one's actions, thoughts, and values into those embodied by the Buddha, Dharma, and Sangha.

The Three Jewels represent ideals that are true for all people at all times, so they embody the dimension of Buddhism that transcends culture. Therefore they provide a way of identifying what in the Buddhist tradition is relevant to today's practitioners. Practising Buddhism means going more and more deeply for

Refuge to the Three Jewels.

Stressing Going for Refuge to the Three Jewels is a way of emphasizing the purpose of the Buddhist path and the spirit that animates it. For the individual Buddhist, Going for Refuge to the Three Jewels means seeing one's life in a mythic context, in which one acts against the backdrop of these timeless truths and strives to realize them for oneself. This contrasts with the materialist and historicist world-view offered by secular society. So far as the FWBO is concerned, all its practices, teachings, and institutions are intended as aids on the path and the means by which to go for Refuge more deeply.

Shrine at Tiratanaloka Retreat Centre

This is not to say that the FWBO does not have to guard against institutionalization and formalism, but it does so through emphasizing the primary importance of commitment to the ideals of Buddhism enacted in Going for Refuge.

GETTING BACK TO BASICS

Sangharakshita's stress on Going for Refuge is an example of his desire to find the full significance of the Dharma in the core teachings and practices of the Buddhist tradition. Similarly, in expounding the Dharma he emphasizes the basic teachings that are common to all the main schools. Approached in this way the diverse and complex character of the Buddhist tradition is not so important for the individual Buddhist: the Dharma can be expressed in simple formulations such as those describing the human condition and the fundamental elements of the Buddhist path, which are true for all people at all times.

The 'recommended reading' towards the end of this book lists material that outlines in detail how the FWBO presents the teachings of the Buddhist tradition. Most of these basic teachings go back to the historical Buddha and are universally relevant. Going for Refuge to the Three Jewels is a possibility for everyone, wherever they live, and the key teachings of Buddhism

tell simple but profound truths about existence. These teachings emphasize being mindful and loving at all times, examining actions in the light of ethical values, and understanding how one's thoughts condition one's life. They are just as relevant in the modern West as they were in medieval Japan or ancient India.

Sangharakshita also emphasizes basic Buddhist practices. If we are to make real spiritual progress we need to start at the beginning. Although it is tempting to dive straight into 'advanced' meditation practices, it is unrealistic to do so and can be confusing. So FWBO centres teach meditation practices that develop a calm, concentrated, and emotionally positive mind, and they stress the importance of friendship, Right Livelihood, and ethics. These teachings and practices are familiar to all Buddhists but they possess great profundity.

As the Buddha's central teachings are explored, they connect with the great Buddhist qualities of wisdom and compassion. And sincere engagement with basic Buddhist practices offers a context for understanding and engaging with the metaphysical teachings of Buddhism. As Sangharakshita asserts: 'There are no higher teachings, only deeper realizations.'

LEARNING FROM THE WHOLE BUDDHIST TRADITION

The FWBO's approach to the Buddhist tradition is radical in the sense that it gets back to the animating spirit and foundational teachings. This means that it does not have to accept some parts and reject others. Any element of that tradition can be a source of inspiration to the extent that it is an expression of the Dharma. Indeed, people in the modern world may be said to be heirs to the whole of Buddhism – that incomparable store of spiritual experience and guidance.

The sources of inspiration are many, and different things can be learned from the scriptures, teachers, and example of the different Buddhist schools. So the FWBO draws from many schools in the service of its re-expression of Buddhism for today. And yet, if we are to avoid confusion, our practice of the Dharma needs to be clear and systematic, so the FWBO has a coherent and well worked-out approach to practice, drawing systematically on particular techniques, texts, and teachings.

The Sevenfold Puja, the movement's basic devotional liturgy, is an example of this combination of flexibility and rigour. This puja is centred on verses from a Mahayana text, the *Bodhicaryavatara*, but it also contains Pali verses, the Refuges and Precepts, that come from the Theravada, and mantras that come from the Vajrayana. The puja as a whole is a coherent and harmonious ritual that enacts an engagement with the principal issues of the spiritual life.

In drawing on the tradition in this way the FWBO follows the example of Buddhists throughout history who have been flexible and pragmatic in communicating Buddhist teachings, yet have remained true to its core teachings and values.

The FWBO's emphasis on the essential spiritual orientation of Buddhism, its core teachings, and its openness to the whole Buddhist tradition, enables it to take a flexible and exploratory approach to understanding what Buddhism should look like in the modern world. The Buddhist movement that is described in the following pages is the product of these explorations.

A spiritual community

A NETWORK OF FRIENDSHIPS

Ananda, the Buddha's friend and personal assistant, once said to the Buddha that half the spiritual life consists of *kalyana mitrata* – spiritual friendship, or friendship with what is lovely. The Buddha replied, `Say not so Ananda, say not so. It is the whole, not the half, of the spiritual life.' The Friends of the Western Buddhist Order takes these words to heart. *Kalyana mitrata*, one might say, is the whole of the FWBO.

All of us need other people to learn from, and relationships that are characterized by honesty and openness. In living a spiritual life we need the friendship of others doing the same, and especially of people who are more experienced. This is referred to in the Buddhist tradition as *kalyana mitrata* or spiritual friendship. There is also a natural need for friendships with peers, and, in time, a wish to befriend those less experienced on the path than oneself. Friendship is not just something that happens naturally when we are with people we like – it is a practice, and it can be a path. Developing friendships and learning to be a true friend means overcoming selfishness, and knowing oneself, as well as knowing others. And it means developing the qualities of a true friend such as generosity, courage, sensitivity, kindness, clarity, patience, and forgiveness. The movement's structures and institutions can all be seen as frameworks for *kalyana mitrata* and friendship.

This spirit of friendship springs naturally from the practice of metta bhavana, the development of loving-

kindness meditation. Metta is an emotion of non-possessive and non-exclusive warmth and affection, so it contrasts with romantic love, just as friendship contrasts with sexual and romantic relationships.

The FWBO's emphasis on friendship has many practical consequences. The art of authentic and open communication is highly valued, and people put time and effort into developing and deepening their friendships. This emphasis is the reason for the development of residential communities and team-based working situations. Sharing one's living or working life with other Buddhists creates excellent conditions for friendships. As most deep friendships (as opposed to romantic attachments) develop between members of the same sex, many FWBO activities are structured along single-sex lines.

FWBO centres are not simply places for teaching the techniques of meditation or imparting information about Buddhism. Everyone who attends an FWBO activity is thought of as a 'Friend', an individual with his or her own needs and path. For those who want it, there exists the opportunity to get to know others at the centre, especially members of the Western Buddhist Order, and to form spiritual friendships with them.

THE WESTERN BUDDHIST ORDER

At the heart of the Friends of the Western Buddhist Order is the Western Buddhist Order (WBO) itself, a spiritual community of men and women who have committed themselves to practising the Dharma. Order members have made Going for Refuge to the Buddha, Dharma, and Sangha the centre of their lives. In particular, they have chosen the Order as the context in which they are trying to do this. And Order members are committed to creating a true spiritual community based on harmony, friendship, and shared endeavour.

A distinctive feature of the WBO is that it is a unified spiritual community, in the sense that it does not make artificial divisions between its members. Membership is open to all, irrespective of age, sex, race, class, caste, or any other such criterion. People are involved simply as individuals. In particular, an order in which men and women are members on the same terms and with equal status, though not unique, is something of an innovation in Buddhist history. Men and women Order members take the same precepts, and practise on an equal basis.

The Order is also distinctive in being neither lay nor monastic. In many Asian Buddhist cultures the Buddhist community or sangha is divided between monks who are seen as the 'real' full-time Buddhists and lay people who often have a lower status. Yet monasticism is a way of life, and does not necessarily denote a particular

Left
photograph by
Prabhakara

Above & left
**Life at Padmaloka
Retreat Centre,
Norfolk**

Newly-ordained women with their preceptors, Il Convento di Santa Croce, Tuscany 1998

courtesy Rupavati

level of spiritual commitment or development. The Western Buddhist Order is open to any man or woman who is sincerely and effectively committed to the Buddhist path, and although Order members try to lead a Buddhist life that is fully committed to practising the Dharma, they are not necessarily monks or nuns. How an Order member lives should be an expression of the commitment they have made, but an individual's lifestyle will depend on their needs, wishes, and circumstances. The crucial thing is the spiritual commitment Order members have made, not the lifestyle they follow. The maxim on which the Order is based is that `commitment is primary and lifestyle secondary'. At one end of the spectrum some Order members have families, while at the other end some are chaste monastics known as *anagarikas*. However, this does not denote a difference in status so much as a difference in context and lifestyle (though this may also reflect a different intensity of practice). The Buddhist ideal is the overcoming of craving and attachment, and Sangharakshita holds up a chaste and simple life – based on detachment from possessions, craving, and sexual activity – as an ideal towards which all Buddhists should be actively working. But it is for each individual to find out for themself how to move towards living in that way.

Becoming an Order member

Ordination is a lifelong commitment and a serious step, so it usually takes several years to become ready for ordination. Anyone can ask for ordination, and then attend the retreats that make up the ordination training course. These retreats are held around the world, and in the UK there are two retreat centres (Padmaloka for men and Tiratanaloka for women) dedicated to running this course. There are currently over a thousand people worldwide who have requested ordination and are engaged in the ordination training process. Ordinations are performed by a senior Order member known as a Preceptor, usually in the context of a special retreat. Guhyaloka Retreat Centre, in a mountain valley in south-eastern Spain, is the setting for two four-month-long retreats a year during which men are ordained. Women's ordination retreats take place in a former Augustinian friary in Tuscany, and fundraising is under way for a full-time facility.

Nobody is ever refused ordination, but people are asked to spend time preparing. Ordination is a commitment that requires self-knowledge as well as experience of the Buddhist path and effective friendships with Order members. Order members at FWBO centres, as well the members of dedicated ordination teams, help women and men to prepare, and assess their readiness.

At ordination, men become Dharmacharis and women Dharmacharinis, meaning `farers in the Dharma'. They make a decisive commitment to Going for Refuge to the Three Jewels, and undertake to follow a traditional set of ten ethical guidelines, which Order members follow as precepts. They also take up a meditation practice which consists in contemplating the visualized image of a Buddha or Bodhisattva. These derive from Tibetan practices, but they are not seen as Tantric *sadhanas* so much as explorations of Going for Refuge in

relation to the Buddhas and Bodhisattvas. The person being ordained is also given a new name by their Preceptor. This is a traditional practice in Buddhism and the names are taken from Pali and Sanskrit, the chief scriptural languages of Indian Buddhism. Each name has a meaning, often reflecting qualities of Enlightenment, so one's name is a symbolic link with one's goal in following the Buddhist path. For instance, `Vishvapani' means `he who holds the universe in his hand', and it is the name of a figure in the Mahayana pantheon of Bodhisattvas. In mid-2000 the Order had 880 members in over twenty countries – around 520 in the UK, 210 in India, and the rest spread around the world. There are currently between 70 and 80 ordinations each year.

What do Order members do?

Ordination means committing oneself to making the Dharma the decisive factor in one's life. But Dharma practice is not simply an individual affair: Order members are also committed to creating a true spiritual fellowship, and there are many opportunities for them to spend time together. The Order is organized into local chapters of up to twelve people, and these meet weekly. These are `spiritual workshops' where people share their insights and difficulties, and

above
Ordination at Padmaloka
photograph by Prabhakara

Left
Ordination in Bhaja in India
photograph by Devamitra

try to help one another in their Dharma practice. In the UK there are regional gatherings on the first weekend of each month, and every two years there is a convention of Order members from around the world. Some Order members live together in communities, and they may work together. Above all they try to share their spiritual lives, and co-operate in spreading and practising the Dharma.

Order members are under no obligation to perform any functions within the FWBO, but it is natural for people following the Dharma to want to share its benefits. Classes at FWBO centres are led by Order members, as are retreats and other events. Order members in FWBO centres see themselves as Dharma practitioners who share what they have learned, rather than as professional Buddhist `teachers' with a role and status superior to and apart from their students. Their aim in teaching is to communicate the Dharma and to create spiritual community among those attending the centre.

How does the Order function?
Because the WBO is free of formal distinctions between its members it is possible for Order members to relate to each other as individuals, not in terms of their status or rank. Naturally, those with more experience are accorded particular respect, but

the Order is a remarkably harmonious body of individuals who are seriously committed to following the Buddha's path.

There are no rules in the Order. Buddhism is a path of individual practice that entails acting for the good because one has taken responsibility for one's thoughts and actions. The Order aims to be a free association of individuals working towards a common goal, and it is founded on the principle that you cannot create spiritual community by force. Therefore, all decisions made by bodies within the Order are made by consensus and according to the ethical precepts.

When difficulties arise, Order members work together to restore harmony and see that, if necessary, restitution is made. In very rare cases where there has been a serious ethical breach and the bonds of spiritual fellowship that define the Order have been broken, an individual's continued membership has sometimes become untenable. But apart from such exceptional cases, resolving difficulties through kind and honest communication is part of the practice of the Order.

THE MITRA SANGHA
When a person first attends a FWBO centre they are considered a `Friend'. They may take part in all the public

activities of the centre, including meditation classes and courses, classes devoted to Buddhist study and practice, festivals, arts events, and so on. There is no obligation or pressure to take their involvement further, and some people remain as Friends – attending a centre and going on retreat on an *ad hoc* basis – for many years. However, as someone's practice of the Dharma deepens, and their connections strengthen, it is possible to formalize this involvement with the work of the Order by becoming a Mitra.

`Mitra' is the Sanskrit word for `friend'. A Mitra is someone who wants to practise Buddhism seriously according to the FWBO's approach, and intends to do so for the foreseeable future.

Together, Order members and Mitras make up the core of the sangha, or spiritual community, around an FWBO centre.

Study at Padmaloka

and the growing maturity of the Order. Nowadays, more advanced FWBO retreats, as well as most communities and teams in Right Livelihood businesses, are either for men or for women. The communities are an alternative to living with a partner or in a family, and the friendships that develop are an emotionally satisfying alternative to the romantic and sexual relationships that naturally develop (at least for the heterosexual majority) within mixed environments.

Single-sex activities go against the norms of most Western social activities, yet they have been a great success, and are usually highly attractive to people becoming involved in the FWBO. Various reasons have been proposed to account for this, but the crux is the experience of what works best. This has been that the sharing, trust, and communication characteristic of a spiritual community is more easily developed with members of one's own sex. In particular it seems that, in general, women can develop friendships most easily and most deeply with other women, and men with other men. This does not imply that one should relate exclusively to members of one's own sex or that friendship and communication is not possible and valuable across the sexes. But it seems that the FWBO's success in developing spiritual community owes much to single-sex activities.

SINGLE-SEX ACTIVITIES

In the Buddhist tradition it has always been common practice for the sexes to meet separately for intensive practice of the Dharma, and the FWBO's experience has led it to adopt this pattern in many of its activities.

In the movement's early days activities were mixed. In the early seventies, people began experimenting with retreats for men and women separately. Most people (often to their own surprise) found them more satisfying because they were relatively free of sexual tension and distraction, and because with members of their own sex they found it easier to be wholly themselves.

Single-sex activities developed in an experimental way. Sometimes there have been difficulties through either men or women feeling excluded from activities for the other sex, and sometimes it has been difficult for Order members to provide the same level of activity for both men and women. But in general these difficulties have been resolved with time, effort,

Ta'i chi ch'uan on retreat at Dhanakosa in Scotland

An engagement with society

SOCIETY AND THE DHARMA

Social context is an issue in the spiritual life. How we live and work has a crucial effect on our states of mind and on our ability to engage in practices such as meditation; more broadly, the society in which we live structures human relationships and has a strong influence on our values. The conditions that exist in the modern Western world are very different from those that have existed in the traditional societies of Asia, so people wishing to practise Buddhism in contemporary society need to understand the world in which they live, and to consider what helps and what hinders their spiritual lives.

A Buddhist critique of modern society is beyond the scope of this book, but it is worth pondering where our views, values, and expectations come from. Europe and North America have societies in which consumer capitalism is the most powerful force; where traditional families have become nuclear families and these are fragmenting in their turn; where technology is progressing rapidly and consumerism is powerful. These forces affect us and structure our lives, whether we like it or not.

These are serious concerns for people in the FWBO, and it is important that the social dimension of Buddhists' lives expresses the difference in their orientation from the values that `make the world go round'. Order members and others in the movement try to base their lives on generosity rather than materialism; contentment rather than acquisitiveness and distraction; and simplicity rather than busyness. Some do this while working in regular jobs and living in a family. Others have developed new ways of living and working together that are alternatives to mainstream society. In the UK, where these alternatives are best established, around half of all Order members and Mitras are involved with them. These alternatives can be seen as the seeds of a new society, one that grows from the values of the Dharma and is concerned with spiritual freedom, selflessness, and Awakening.

LIFESTYLES

In traditional Buddhist countries the issue of lifestyle has arisen as a simple choice between being a monk, or nun, or a lay person. The monastic code determined the lives of monks and nuns, and the lives of lay Buddhists generally followed the pattern of their societies. Because Order members are not bound to a particular lifestyle they have had the flexibility to explore how the Dharma may best be followed in the fluid conditions of modernity.

Sukhavati community, London
photograph by Vincent Stokes

Residential communities

Across Britain, and other countries where FWBO activities have taken root, are scattered over a hundred residential FWBO communities. Some are located above an FWBO centre, others are in quiet houses in the suburbs, or in city-centre flats. The largest communities house up to twenty, and the smallest have just three or four individuals living together.

Community life is a practice, so these FWBO communities are far more than shared houses. Sharing one's life with spiritual friends is fulfilling because of the opportunity it offers to create along with others a context for meditation, mindfulness, communication, and friendship.

Sometimes people share a room, and sometimes everyone has a room of their own, but there is usually a communal shrine-room. A typical day in an FWBO community might start with a group meditation, when the community members sit together in silence. Then comes breakfast, and a chance to tune in. In some communities people work together as well as live together, which makes for greater intensity of shared experience. Some communities are part of an FWBO centre where residents may work, or in a retreat centre where the community will also include the team that runs retreats. At least one night a

week residents might gather for a community meeting, which may be a time of shared ritual or meditation practice, or a chance to communicate one's experience, struggles, and discoveries. Naturally there are sometimes difficulties and conflicts as a result of living in such close proximity, but engaging with these constructively, and learning to overcome differences, is one of the most valuable aspects of the practice of communal living.

FWBO communities vary in their intensity and focus, and it is always up to the residents to decide how they want to live. For instance, some are open to boyfriends and girlfriends staying overnight, whilst others are not. Because they are contexts in which individuals come together to practise the Buddhist path based on sharing and a communal lifestyle, they consist of single people, not couples. This is an important reason for their being almost always either for men or for women.

Practising in a family

Many of those who became involved in the movement in the UK in its early days were young, single people without prior commitments or responsibilities. For them, single-sex communities offered an ideal context for committed practice. But a somewhat different pattern has been seen in the movement's development in countries

Dharmacharini Srimati with her son
photograph by Vincent Stokes

such as the US and Australia, and over time the demographic profile of people involved in the FWBO in the UK has changed. The first generation has grown to middle age and people who become involved in the FWBO thirty years into its history come from a wide range of ages and backgrounds. Naturally, there are now many people involved in the movement (including many Order members) who have families. Indeed, in India this is true of the great majority of Order members. For those who live in a family the challenge is to make it a supportive environment for Dharma practice – one that conduces to generosity, simplicity, and non-attachment. The existence of single-sex classes, retreats, and study groups at FWBO centres offers parents an opportunity to be with spiritual friends and experience the benefits of an undistracted environment, away from the pressures of child-care and family life. However, this is not always enough, and as the membership of the FWBO has diversified a range of supportive conditions has been developing to help those who live in families. Festivals are opportunities for family activities, and centres often provide crèches and activities for children on these days. Family retreats are a regular occurrence, there are parents' groups at many FWBO centres, and there is a publication for families called *Jataka*.

Sex and chastity

In his Four Noble Truths, one of the most basic expressions of the Dharma, the Buddha taught that craving is the crucial cause of the frustration, unhappiness, and suffering of our lives. So the Buddhist path involves overcoming craving and becoming more content. Sex is perhaps the most compelling focus for our craving, and when we feel discontented there is a strong tendency to look to sex and sexual partners – whether actual or fantasized. So practising the Dharma means developing an inner life of stillness and creativity, and becoming less oriented towards sex. Although the WBO is not a celibate Order, sex is still an issue in the spiritual lives of its members. The practice of abstention from sexual activity is increasingly emphasized within the Order, as something to work towards by becoming increasingly contented and self-aware. Some Order members are married, some are single, and some are celibate; some are `gay' and some are `straight', and the same ethical and spiritual principles apply in each case. It is important that we are aware of our motivations with regard to sex, and that we do not act in a manipulative way or one that harms others. A growing number of Order members have become *anagarikas*, which means they have adopted a monastic lifestyle based on chastity, simplicity, community living, and fewness of possessions.

RIGHT LIVELIHOOD BUSINESSES

Everyone needs financial support, and most of us spend a good deal of our lives working. The work we do has a strong effect on our minds, and Right Livelihood is the traditional Buddhist term for work that is ethical and helpful to one's spiritual development. In the 1970s people in the movement started working together as a way of raising money to support themselves and fund Buddhist projects. They soon discovered that work could itself be a means of spiritual practice, a training ground for awareness, and the capacity to co-operate and take initiative.

There are now many `team-based Right Livelihood businesses'. These can be seen as a social and economic experiment conducted on a substantial scale, creating a new approach to work, money, and property that reflects Buddhist values. From one point of view, they are heirs to the socialist and communitarian projects of the last two centuries. From another, they parallel the socially engaged Buddhism that is developing in some Asian countries. They can also be seen as a unique re-expression of Buddhism.

The success of FWBO Right Livelihood ventures is best seen in the largest of these businesses, Windhorse Trading, which imports crafts, gifts, and houseware and sells them wholesale and through a chain of shops. Around a hundred people work in the company's Cambridge headquarters – busy offices and several warehouses piled high with goods. The boxes and pallets are interspersed with shrines and Buddha images, reminders of the purpose of the business and safeguards against becoming lost in the busyness of daily operations. Most of the workers live communally in houses in the centre of Cambridge. They start their working day with a dedication ceremony, and their routine is interspersed with

Members of the Gallery Cafe team, London
photograph by Vincent Stokes

meetings that explore how the work could be a more effective spiritual practice and help the workers to stay in good communication with each other.

The warehouses hum with activity – loading, unloading, and sorting – and the offices are filled with people taking orders for goods and administering this sizeable operation, but there is a prevailing atmosphere of calm and concentration, as well as of lightness, humour, and creativity. A large new FWBO centre in Cambridge has been bought thanks to Windhorse Trading's success. It includes a Georgian theatre that, among other things, hosts performances by a choir and a theatre group made up of people who work at Windhorse. Another hundred people work for Windhorse Trading in 'Evolution' shops around the UK, as well as Ireland, Spain, and Germany. Each of these shops is connected with an FWBO centre and staffed by members of the local sangha. They offer an opportunity for committed Dharma practice, and profits from the shops can be used to help the local centre. Right Livelihood ventures such as Windhorse Trading differ from ordinary businesses in several respects.

Firstly, they provide a reasonable level of financial support for their workers, but they do not pay wages or salaries.

The level of support is worked out according to people's personal circumstances and needs. For example, a parent may need more support than a single person living in a community. The businesses also provide several weeks' paid retreat time a year for each worker. This sustains a lifestyle that values simplicity and contentment, rather than the acquisition of material possessions.

Secondly, they engage only in work that is ethical. Right Livelihood businesses avoid products that cause harm to people or the environment, and where possible concentrate on those that are beneficial to the world. For example, FWBO businesses contributed to the popularization of vegetarianism in the UK, while Windhorse Trading develops 'fair trade' links with suppliers in the Third World.

Thirdly, they offer a context for spiritual friendship. Working with someone on a common project is perhaps the best way to get to know them – especially if one also lives with them. In a Buddhist workplace the development of more kindness, patience, and mindfulness is an immediate, day-to-day, and shared concern.

Finally, these businesses give away their profits. Some of the businesses have

been set up to finance their local FWBO centres. Others help to seed new projects or help existing ones that rely on donations (such as some publishing ventures, and retreat centres). FWBO Right Livelihood businesses have given money to help Indian slum-dwellers, children of Tibetan refugees, and other causes.

Right Livelihood hasn't been easy. Many FWBO businesses were started with more idealism than money, and more willingness than expertise. But there has been dramatic progress and there are now many working situations that are both personally and spiritually satisfying and competitive in the business world.

SOCIAL ACTION
As well as developing its own structures and institutions, people within the FWBO also want to help society at large. Firstly, they are citizens, and Sangharakshita has emphasized the importance of playing a full role in civic life. Institutionally the FWBO makes a contribution to society through its meditation classes, businesses, and other activities. And many Order members help others through their jobs as doctors, teachers, psychologists, and social workers.

The movement's work in India has dimensions of both Dharma teaching

and social work. When activities started there in 1978 it soon became clear that simply teaching Buddhism was not enough. There was a need for material help, and a charity, Bahujan Hitay (`for the welfare of the many') was set up to run social-work projects. These projects in education, medicine, and culture, are now spreading throughout India.

The main educational project is a network of hostels for children who would otherwise have no schooling. Other projects include kindergartens and adult literacy classes as well as non-formal education classes. Medical projects include a health centre and a number of slum-based community health schemes. Cultural activities include the Ashvaghosha Project, which uses story-telling techniques to explore issues relevant to local communities, and karate classes for children, which help greatly in their developing self-esteem.

Most of the work carried out by Bahujan Hitay is funded by the Karuna Trust, a UK charity set up by Order members specifically to fund social projects in India and elsewhere. Karuna also funds projects outside Bahujan Hitay that help with health and education among Buddhists and others, including Tibetan refugees in the Indian subcontinent.

CREATING A NEW BUDDHIST CULTURE

In every country where Buddhism has flourished Buddhists have created works of art expressing their faith. Indeed, whole cultures – from ancient India to medieval Japan – have flourished under the influence of Buddhism. This suggests that there is a strong natural relationship between the Buddhist spiritual life and the practice of the arts. The inner life that unfolds through Buddhist practice can find expression in the images of painting and the metaphors of poetry, as only such intuitive and suggestive media can adequately express its values and sensibilities. Practice and appreciation of the arts are themselves means of cultivating the mind. In many Asian countries Buddhism has helped create whole cultures that are, to some extent, imbued with the values of the Dharma. The arts express those values concretely and publicly.

But it is not enough for Westerners simply to encounter the images and literature of the Buddhist East. Western culture has its own artistic traditions that have created the `language' of the Western imagination, and the great images and themes of that culture have done much to inform Western sensibilities. They are a repository of values, perceptions, and sensibility that speak directly to Western minds, and

suggests that for Buddhism to be firmly rooted in the West it must learn to speak the `language' of Western culture. He sees the task for Western Buddhists to be the creation of a new Buddhist culture: one that is genuinely Buddhist but not culturally foreign to the West.

Both Western culture and Buddhism are vast and hugely varied. A key to engaging with both as an aspect of the Buddhist path is the imagination: the mode of being in which one perceives life in its wholeness, with both intellect and emotion, through images and metaphors. Imagination is a faculty that can be developed and refined, and it is connected with the traditional Buddhist faculties of faith and wisdom: ways of experiencing that go far beyond concepts or feelings. The practice and appreciation of the arts can help to enlarge the imagination, opening gateways to greater awareness, so by immersing oneself in myth, symbol, great music, literature, and the visual arts one can find a language for the apprehension of the spiritual life: some of the greatest Western artists, poets, and writers have had apprehensions of the meditative states and insights to which Buddhist practice leads.

Appreciation and practice of the arts has always been seen within the FWBO as an important means of engaging the

sometimes parallel the insights of Buddhism. These traditions are a resource on which Western Buddhists can draw and from which they can learn, alongside their practice of Buddhism. Therefore Sangharakshita

practice and appreciation of the arts in their programmes of events. Many individuals, while not full-time artists, benefit from the writers' groups, poetry readings, life classes, and other events that are held in FWBO centres, or they follow Sangharakshita's example of engaging with Western art and literature whilst also studying Buddhist texts and teachings, and practising meditation.

These activities are hardly the `Second Renaissance' that Schopenhauer predicted might arise from the impact of the Wisdom of the East upon Western civilization. But they might be seen as the germ of a culture that could arise in the West that is an expression of Buddhist practice and sensibility, yet speaks in a Western idiom.

These phrases – `seeds of a new society', `germ of a Western Buddhist culture' – suggest that the ambitious process that has been initiated in the FWBO is an organic one. Over the years, perhaps the centuries, the effects of bringing together serious engagement with the Dharma and the social and cultural conditions of the modern world may have a transforming effect. This aspiration – and the image of a spiritually vital culture dedicated to the highest values and potentials of human life – is a vital inspiration behind the FWBO.

Oracle Dance Co.
photograph
© MalcolmHolmes

emotions in the spiritual life. There are many working artists, musicians, and writers within the FWBO. Some produce traditional Buddhist images, and these are gradually becoming more Western in appearance and `feel'; others are working within the Western traditions. Works that truly deserve to be called expressions of a new Buddhist culture will only be produced as a result of the labours of individual artists over many years.

There is also a communal dimension to artistic engagement in the FWBO. 1993 saw the opening of two FWBO arts centres, and FWBO centres often include

A path of Buddhist practice

Buddhism teaches a path of spiritual transformation. The FWBO draws on the reservoir of the Buddhist tradition to offer a systematic, coherent, and effective approach to that path. Meditation is at the heart of its life and teaching, but it is not the only method for changing oneself. If the changes brought about by the Dharma are to be genuine and lasting, the whole of one's life should be affected.

One principle behind the FWBO's approach to spiritual development is the need to develop a range of balancing qualities, such as the `five spiritual faculties': faith, wisdom, mindfulness, energy, and meditation. Some practices relate more directly to the development of one or other of these qualities, and the range of practices followed within the FWBO helps to ensure that individuals' development is not one-sided, or a reflection of a temperamental bias.

A second principle is that there are both direct and indirect ways of transforming the mind. Meditation is the most direct method, because in meditation the mind changes itself. But many other activities can have a positive, even transforming, effect through less direct means: friendship, Right Livelihood, and the arts can all be seen as practices in this sense. So as well as meditating, many individuals within the FWBO practise disciplines such as t'ai chi ch'uan, hatha yoga, and karate. FWBO centres often hold yoga classes, and their arts activities, events exploring human communication, and similar activities can be seen as teaching other indirect methods of development. But because these activities do not form part of the `core curriculum' of the FWBO's approach to Dharma practice, they will not be described in detail here.

Thirdly, Dharma practice needs to be regular and systematic. Some people are attracted to Buddhism from a desire for spiritual or psychic attainments. But genuine and lasting change means getting to grips with the whole of one's experience. As Sangharakshita puts it, people coming to Buddhism may start by feeling attracted to advanced practices, but eventually they need to follow the `path of regular steps', starting with the most basic elements of Buddhist practice, and building up from there.

The areas of practice that are taught at every FWBO centre and followed by all Order members and Mitras are ethics, meditation, devotional ritual, and study of the Dharma.

ETHICS

To live is to act, and our actions can have consequences that are either harmful or beneficial to others and ourselves. Buddhist ethics means acting with an awareness of this truth – seeing that our actions have consequences, and learning the skill of acting for the best. The Buddha did not lay down sets of rules governing how we should act in every instance. Instead, he emphasized the importance of considering what drives us to act in a particular way and purifying our hearts and minds through practices such as meditation. For Buddhists, ethics is less about doing good than being good.

Lest we should lose ourselves in a maze of self-analysis, the Buddha also proposed five basic guidelines. If we keep to these, he suggested, we won't go far wrong. These are the five precepts that all Buddhists undertake to follow, and everyone seriously involved with the FWBO considers it very important to adhere to them.

1. *Not killing or causing harm to other living beings.* This is the fundamental ethical principle for Buddhists, and all the other precepts are elaborations of this one. The precept implies acting non-violently wherever possible, and people in the FWBO are vegetarian for this reason. The positive counterpart of this precept is acting with compassion.

2. *Not taking that which has not been given.* Stealing is an obvious way in which one can harm others. One can also take advantage of, exploit, or manipulate people – all these can be seen as ways of taking the not-given. The positive counterpart of this precept is generosity, which is greatly stressed as an important Buddhist virtue.

3. *Avoiding sexual misconduct.* This precept has been interpreted in many ways over time, but essentially it means not causing harm to others or oneself through one's sexual activity. The positive counterpart of this precept is contentment.

4. *Avoiding false speech.* Speech is the crucial element in our relations with others, yet language is a slippery medium; we often deceive others or ourselves without even realizing what we are doing. Truthfulness, the positive counterpart of this precept, is therefore essential to an ethical life.

5. *Abstaining from intoxicants that cloud the mind.* The positive counterpart of this precept is mindfulness, or awareness. Mindfulness is a fundamental quality to be developed on the Buddha's path, and experience shows that the taking of intoxicating drink or drugs runs directly counter to this.

Many Buddhists around the world recite the five precepts every day, and try to put them into practice in their lives. They are `principles of training' that are undertaken freely and need to be applied with intelligence and sensitivity. The Buddhist tradition acknowledges that life is complex and throws up many difficulties, and it does not suggest that there is a single course of action that will be right in all circumstances. It is for the individual to implement the precepts with responsibility, awareness, and integrity. The traditional word that describes ethical actions is *kushala*, which literally means `skilful'. Such actions are motivated by love, generosity, and compassion, while unethical or *akushala* actions are motivated by greed, hatred, and delusion. Learning to be ethical, then, is a skill or an art, something one learns, a faculty one seeks to refine.

A true ethical sensibility develops as one becomes more aware of oneself and others through reflection and open communication. Spiritual friends are important here. Indeed, part of the value of sangha or spiritual community is that others will point out the lapses of which one is unaware or would like to avoid, and the example of their personal lives will, ideally at least, be an inspiration to change for the better.

The importance of ethics in the spiritual life is stressed throughout the FWBO. Mitras are asked to follow the five precepts, and all Order members follow a similar list of ten precepts.

MEDITATION

Buddhism has developed many methods for working on the mind, but meditation is the most important. Buddhist meditation practices are ways of developing concentration, clarity, and emotional positivity. Meditation teaches one the patterns and habits of the mind, and serious and regular meditation is a way to cultivate new, more positive states such as calm, concentration, and awareness, and emotions like loving-kindness (or *metta*), compassion, and equanimity. With discipline and patience the positive, calm, and focused states of meditative awareness can become profoundly tranquil and energized. Using the awareness developed in meditation it is possible to gain a fuller understanding of oneself, other people, and life itself.

Over the millennia countless meditation practices have been developed in the Buddhist tradition. All of them may be described as `mind-trainings', but they take many approaches. The foundation of all Buddhist meditation, however, is the cultivation of a calm and positive state of mind.

Learning meditation

Each year thousands of people learn

47

meditation at FWBO centres. They learn two basic meditations that develop these qualities: the mindfulness of breathing and the loving-kindness meditation or *metta bhavana*.

As techniques, these meditation practices are very simple. However, reading about them is no substitute for learning from an experienced and reliable teacher who can offer guidance in how to apply the technique and deal with difficulties. Perhaps most importantly, a teacher can offer the encouragement and inspiration of their own example.

At FWBO centres meditation is taught by Order members who are experienced meditators. Classes and courses are open to everyone and you need not be interested in Buddhism to learn. Motives for taking up meditation vary. Some people want to improve their concentration for work, study, or sports; others are looking for calm and peace of mind. Then there are people trying to answer fundamental questions about life. Meditation works on all these levels. Calm and concentrated meditative states have psychological benefits, but they are also well suited to penetrating the truth – and that is the ultimate goal of Buddhist practice.

Meditators at Padmaloka Retreat Centre, Norfolk
photograph by Prabhakara

The mindfulness of breathing

As its name implies, the mindfulness of breathing (*anapanasati* in Pali) uses the breath as an object of concentration, and the practice takes one through four stages that require progressively greater attention. By focusing on the breath one becomes aware of the mind's tendency to jump from one thing to another. The simple discipline of concentration brings one back to the present moment and all the richness of experience it contains. It is a way to develop mindfulness, the faculty of alert and sensitive awareness. And it is an excellent method for cultivating the states of intense meditative absorption known as *dhyana* that form the basis for seeing things as they really are. The mindfulness of breathing is an effective antidote to restlessness and anxiety and a good way to relax: concentration on the breath has a tonic effect on one's entire physical and mental state.

The development of loving-kindness

The Pali name of this practice is *metta bhavana*. *Metta* means 'love' in a non-romantic sense of the word, friendliness, or kindness: hence `loving-kindness' for short. *Metta* is an emotion, and it is felt in the heart. *Bhavana* means development or cultivation. The commonest form of the practice is in five stages, each of which lasts about five minutes for a beginner.

In the first stage, you feel *metta* for yourself, becoming aware of yourself and focusing on feelings of peace, calm, and tranquillity. Then these grow into happiness and love, perhaps with the aid of an image like golden light, or phrases such as `May I be well and happy, may I progress.' Such non-egotistical self-love is a vital basis for emotional positivity. In the second stage you think of a good friend and, using an image, a phrase, or simply the feeling of love, develop *metta* towards them. In the third stage *metta* is directed towards someone you do not particularly like or dislike, and in the fourth stage it is directed towards someone you actually dislike. In the last stage, first of all you feel *metta* for all four people together – yourself, the friend, the neutral person, and the enemy. Then you extend the feeling of love from your heart to everyone in the world, to all beings everywhere.

This beautiful meditation practice has a strong effect on the emotional life. It tends to make the meditator friendlier and emotionally stronger – less buffeted by the ups and downs of life. Just as the mindfulness of breathing spills over into the practice of mindfulness, the *metta bhavana* is expressed in communication, friendship, and more positive human relationships.

A system of meditation

The FWBO's approach to teaching meditation is an example of its approach to Buddhism more generally. The practices it teaches are drawn from several traditions, but they are taught progressively and systematically, according to the deepening spiritual needs of individuals.

Only the mindfulness of breathing and the *metta bhavana* are taught in FWBO centres, and these are the main practices up to the point of ordination within the Western Buddhist Order. This is because concentration and emotional positivity are essential bases of meditation.

Ordination is a wholehearted commitment to making the Dharma the centre of one's life. At ordination each person takes on a meditation practice that presupposes such commitment. Order members undertake to meditate on the qualities of a Buddha or Bodhisattva. They may also engage in insight meditation practices such as the contemplation of the insubstantiality of the six elements of the mind and body.

DEVOTION

Because Buddhism is a path of transformation it is not enough to understand it intellectually. Buddhism is reasonable, but practising it effectively demands a response to its ideals and a willingness to put its teachings into effect. Emotional and imaginative engagement are also essential.

Buddhist devotional rituals or pujas offer a focus for cultivating such faith, and pujas are important within the FWBO. They include three main elements: reciting verses, chanting, and making offerings. The verses are associated with the principal tenets and ideals of Buddhism, and give expression to the spiritual aspiration that makes someone a Buddhist. Several liturgies have been drawn from traditional sources or composed more recently. Pujas are a regular feature of the life of FWBO centres, a focus for the sangha to come together in collective expression of their shared aspirations.

STUDYING THE BUDDHA'S TEACHINGS

For the Buddha's teachings to take you to Enlightenment, Buddhist tradition says you must do three things: listen, reflect, and meditate on them.

First it is important to know what Buddhism teaches. The Buddha had a radical and distinctive approach to life, which underlies meditation and other Buddhist practices. Talks and courses, which are held at every FWBO centre, are opportunities to hear the Dharma in this way. Many centres also have bookshops with texts from across the Buddhist tradition.

Reflecting on the Dharma can be done individually or with others. Study groups are a chance to clarify understanding, share experience, and learn new approaches along with others, so these are an important part of how teaching happens in the FWBO. Mitras follow a three-year study course; study is an important part of the ordination training process, and there is also a course for Order members. Sangharakshita emphasizes that alongside a faithful wish to learn from the Dharma we need a critical awareness of the Buddhist tradition that draws on a range of commentarial material in study, including the findings of modern research, the Buddhist scholarly tradition, and even comparative literature.

The Buddha famously compared his teachings to a raft. They are means of realizing the truth for oneself; just as a raft is a means of crossing a river so meditating on the Dharma is the third stage, because Buddhism aims at an understanding of life that transforms one's entire being. Study in the FWBO often takes place in the context of retreats and seminars, when one can reflect on Buddhist teachings in meditation.

Vajrakuta, in North Wales, is a community and teaching centre dedicated to study. A small community leads a life based on study and reflection on Buddhist and related topics, and its members lead seminars and study weeks on Buddhist philosophy, history, and canonical texts. Other retreat centres such as Taraloka Women's Retreat Centre also offer study retreats. Some people in the FWBO have made extensive studies of aspects of the Buddhist tradition. Sangharakshita is widely respected for his learning and his insight, and a number of Order members and Mitras are respected academic scholars of Buddhism, teaching in universities.

In all these study activities there is an attempt to see the Buddha's teachings in relation to the spiritual life. The Dharma may challenge long-held views, and these challenges offer a basis for prolonged reflection. Just as meditation implies the individual taking responsibility for his or her mind, so study means taking responsibility for one's own views, opinions, and understanding of life, and holding one's ideas and experience up to the light of the Buddha's teaching.

A worldwide Buddhist movement

Since the movement's foundation in 1967, the FWBO has grown steadily into an international movement. There are around sixty-three centres (meaning dedicated premises) in cities around the world, as well as seventeen retreat centres. The FWBO started in the UK, and this is still its principal focus. More than half the members of the WBO live in Britain, which has twenty-one urban FWBO centres and eight retreat centres, plus activities in many other towns. It is one of the largest and most developed Buddhist movements in Britain and an important part of the country's Buddhist community. Activities have spread steadily through western Europe, and there are centres in Ireland, France, the Netherlands,

Belgium, Spain, Germany, Norway, Sweden, and Finland, as well as activities in Portugal, Italy, Greece, Poland, the Czech Republic, Russia, and Estonia.

In the New World, FWBO activities started in the US in 1980 and there are now five centres in the US and Canada, as well as centres in Mexico and Venezuela. Not long after the movement's establishment in the UK, activities began in New Zealand, and later a start was made in Australia. Both countries now have several FWBO centres. In Asia there are FWBO activities in Nepal and Sri Lanka, and above all there are the activities in India, and these are described below, because their size and the difference in their cultural context mean they require separate treatment. There are also some activities in South Africa.

Ensuring harmony and communication between the parts of such a widespread movement has become an important function in itself, and in 1994 a central focus was established in Birmingham in central England, called Madhyamaloka. This is the base for senior men and women Order members who have responsibilities for the FWBO as a whole, and who set a spiritual lead for the movement.

Above
Bor Dhoran Retreat Centre in India
photograph by Devamitra

Left
Council meeting at Aryaloka Retreat Center, New Hampshire

the 'love mode'. This is in contrast to the 'power mode', in which people are forced to do things against their will. In Buddhist ethics this principle is expressed in the first precept: not killing or causing harm to other living beings. The commitment involved in becoming a member of the Order is to act ethically and according to the love mode. So FWBO centres are founded on the principle of operating through co-operation and consensus.

Spiritual commitment is at the core

It is not enough to assert that the FWBO *should* operate through love and not power. It requires people who are committed to making this happen. So it is important that those who control FWBO activities have made an explicit and deep commitment to ethical action in the light of Buddhist teaching. Just such a commitment is made in becoming a member of the Western Buddhist Order, so Order members hold the positions of responsibility in institutions of the FWBO, and have legal control over them. It is their responsibility to ensure that all FWBO activities are expressions of Buddhist values.

Autonomy

The FWBO consists of numerous charities that are legally and financially autonomous. So each FWBO centre is the responsibility of a local FWBO charity. This means that the charity's trustees,

HOW THE FWBO FUNCTIONS

Organizational bodies within the FWBO are not just impersonal institutions. They try to embody the values of Buddhism itself and are carefully based on several mutually balancing principles.

Operating in the 'love mode'

The essence of Buddhist ethics is the attempt to base one's actions on virtues such as kindness, generosity, contentment, honesty, and awareness. Borrowing a phrase from the psychologist Erich Fromm, Sangharakshita calls this way of acting who are Order members involved with that centre, are responsible for what happens at the centre. There is no central authority in the FWBO with the power to issue orders.

Consensus

Decisions within the councils of these autonomous charities are always made by consensus, not by edict or vote. This is sometimes not an easy way to operate, and there can be strong disagreements, but it means that, rather than dissenters being silenced through a vote, issues have to be talked through until there is harmony and understanding.

Spiritual hierarchy

As a spiritual community, the Western Buddhist Order aims to operate as much as possible from wisdom and compassion. Pragmatically within a community it transpires that some members are more experienced and more able to put Buddhist principles into effect than others. Consequently some Order members are highly respected for their experience, maturity, and depth of practice, and their voices are accorded due weight. Each centre council elects a Chairman, an experienced Order member who takes responsibility for its work and offers a spiritual lead.

A similar principle operates in the FWBO as a whole. Order members look to Sangharakshita and senior Order members (particularly those who have responsibilities for the Order and movement as a whole) for spiritual guidance and leadership. Most FWBO centres also choose a President, a senior Order member from outside their situation who is consulted on all major developments. This is a further way of ensuring that each area of the FWBO's work remains in accordance with Buddhist values.

Acting in harmony with the FWBO as a whole

There are regular meetings between Order members who hold similar responsibilities – Chairmen, people with responsibility for the Mitra system, Presidents, and so on. The aim of these meetings is to provide peer support, ensure harmony, run joint projects, and prevent any centre becoming isolated from the rest of the movement.

Experiment

Whilst FWBO centres follow generally the same teachings and practices, there is also a place for experiment. The FWBO is a creative endeavour, a collective attempt to explore how the Buddhist path can best be followed in the modern world. However, it is important that experimentation does not degenerate into change for change's sake. It needs to be conscious, and the results should be carefully assessed. Where innovations are successful and prove to be based soundly on Buddhist principles, they are often copied at other centres.

This is not a definitive list of principles, more a description of the approaches that have emerged from issues that have arisen in the course of the FWBO's development. From some perspectives it can appear to be a large, homogeneous organization, but it is a thriving spiritual community. It has to address many issues of decision-making, organization, and power, but it has consistently maintained its commitment to dealing with these as a sangha operating in accordance with the values of Buddhism. FWBO centres are not free from difficulties, but these principles and the structures that have evolved from them offer means of addressing such difficulties with integrity and in the spirit of sangha.

FWBO CENTRES

The focus for the FWBO in a particular town or city is the local FWBO centre, which runs activities introducing people to meditation and Buddhism. Around the largest and most developed centres, such as those in London and Manchester in the UK, Essen in Germany, or Poona and Nagpur in India, there are many other activities.

London
Buddhist Centre
photograph by
Vincent Stokes

54

The London Buddhist Centre

The London Buddhist Centre (LBC) is one of the largest urban Buddhist centres in the West, and perhaps the best-established FWBO centre. It opened in 1978, in a building that was once a Victorian fire station, and it has become a well-known landmark in the East End of London. The Centre runs a full programme of activities led by Order members, and every week several hundred people pass through its doors. It holds classes and courses in meditation and Buddhism and, for those who are more seriously involved, activities devoted to exploring and practising Buddhism in more depth.

The LBC is the hub of a burgeoning `Buddhist village'. Around 200 people live in residential communities or other situations near the centre, though many from further afield participate in its activities. Some of those living in communities have ordinary jobs, but many work in one or other of the FWBO projects around the Centre. There are several Right Livelihood businesses, including Friends Organic health-food shop, Evolution gift shop, Jambala Bookshop, the Gallery Café, a bric-à-brac shop, and the Wild Cherry vegetarian restaurant. These businesses are run co-operatively as team-based Right Livelihood businesses.

Just down the road is Bodywise Natural

Health Centre, which runs classes in yoga, t'ai chi ch'uan, and Alexander Technique, and offers a wide range of alternative treatments and therapies. The London Buddhist Arts Centre is a focus for practising artists, as well as those with an appreciation of the arts or interested in getting involved with the LBC's choir, drama group, or writing group.

The LBC also owns a retreat centre called Potash Farm in the Suffolk countryside, and each summer and Christmas the centre runs two-week-long retreats in hired premises, which are open to all and can cater for over a hundred people. A distinctive feature of the LBC's activities is the events for specific groups of people. There are courses aimed at gay men and at black people, and the centre has held activities for people who are HIV positive and for the disabled. These outreach activities are ways to make the centre accessible to people who might otherwise think it is not for them. Even though there are several other FWBO centres in London, the LBC regularly runs classes in central London and courses in South London. In all, the LBC's highly skilled meditation teachers teach thousands of people to meditate each year.

Having been in existence for over two decades, the LBC has gradually become part of the local community in this part of London's East End. Buddhists are involved in various aspects of community life, and have friendly relations with local people. Each year at Wesak, the celebration of the Buddha's Enlightenment, the Centre holds a large festival and throws its doors open to all. The restaurant gives away food, and banners decorate the streets.

The LBC attracts people from all walks of life. It is a flourishing and varied community, and a remarkable example of Buddhism establishing itself in the West.

What happens at FWBO centres?

Each FWBO centre organizes its own programme of events, experimenting with what works best, but they all teach broadly the same material, so common patterns of teaching have emerged. The outline of activities that follows is not true for all FWBO centres, but it is typical of most.

INTRODUCTORY ACTIVITIES
FWBO centres teach meditation and Buddhism to newcomers through classes and courses. Teaching in the FWBO is done by members of the Order who are themselves experienced in the practice and study of meditation and Buddhism.

Two views of Manchester Buddhist Centre
photograph by
Moksajyoti
© Clear Vision

There is no expectation that people attending the centre will be Buddhists or even that they will agree with Buddhist teachings. The classes are an opportunity to learn and test out Buddhist practices in the light of one's experience, and in an atmosphere of friendly, encouraging communication.

Open classes offer a brief introduction to meditation. The programme of the evening varies from centre to centre and from week to week, but all the classes teach the mindfulness of breathing and the *metta bhavana*. There may also be a talk on meditation or

Buddhism, time to ask questions and share experiences in smaller, more informal, discussion groups, or another activity that supports the main practice, such as walking meditation.

Meditation courses, usually consisting of weekly classes lasting about six weeks, give an excellent grounding in the principles and practices of meditation. As well as simply learning the basic techniques of meditation, there is much to learn about how to work with those techniques, how to address difficulties, and how meditation relates to daily life. Similarly, Buddhism

courses give a grounding in the main teachings of Buddhism. The courses provide time for discussion and reflection, and the teaching typically involves not just theory but metaphor, myth, and the practical implications of the Buddhist view of life. FWBO centres also hold a range of activities at weekends, from intensive meditation days to study days or workshops on an aspect of the arts. Most FWBO centres run weekend retreats in the country so that newcomers and more experienced practitioners can explore meditation and Buddhism and get to know one another better.

REGULARS' CLASSES AND OTHER ACTIVITIES
Beyond the introductory level, regulars' classes have a more explicitly Buddhist orientation, and include pujas (devotional ceremonies) as well as Dharma talks. These are usually open to anyone with an established meditation practice who wishes to take their involvement further.

Study groups offer ways of exploring Buddhist ideas in theory and practice at greater depth than is possible at a larger class. These are also a chance to get to know teachers and peers, and so make a more personal connection with the centre.

Centres usually have a programme of activities on evenings and at weekends,

RETREATS

Getting away from the distractions and busyness of daily life enables one to engage more fully with meditation, and meditating several times a day means that the benefits of meditation can accumulate and go deeper. A retreat offers excellent conditions in which to explore meditation and Buddhism, to find the space to get to know oneself better, and to break old habits, sometimes making a dramatic breakthrough.

All FWBO centres run retreats, and some have their own country retreat centres. There are also larger retreat centres that cater for people from a wider area. The FWBO runs many different kinds of retreats. Some are for beginners, many concentrate just on meditation, while others focus on yoga, the arts, study, or a similar activity.

The programme for an introductory retreat includes teaching and several periods of meditation practice each day. There are usually also talks, discussion, and the opportunity for walks in the countryside. Some retreats last just a weekend: people are often surprised how strong the transforming effect of meditation and a calm and friendly environment can be in such a short time. Other introductory retreats last a week or longer.

aimed at the various levels of experience, and exploring a range of activities from meditation to study, ritual, and the arts.

FESTIVALS

The Buddha advised his followers that if they were to thrive they should `meet together regularly and in large numbers'. So festivals are central to the life of the FWBO. They provide an opportunity for celebration and the expression of devotion and gratitude to the Buddha and his teachings.

The principal festivals celebrated in the FWBO are devoted to the Three Jewels. Wesak, the celebration of the Buddha's Enlightenment, takes place on the full moon of May. The Buddha's Enlightenment is the central event in Buddhism, and Wesak is the most important festival of the Buddhist year. Dharma Day, the celebration of the Buddha's teaching, takes place on the full moon of July. And Sangha Day in November is a celebration of both the ideal of spiritual community and the actual spiritual community in which one is involved. Many centres also celebrate the festival of Padmasambhava, the legendary teacher who established Buddhism in Tibet with whom Sangharakshita has a strong connection through his teachers, and Parinirvana Day, which marks the death of the Buddha. In April people from many FWBO centres gather for the national celebration of the movement's foundation, known as FWBO Day.

Retreat Centres

Many FWBO retreat centres house communities whose members base their lives around meditation or study, and run programmes connected with their own practice. Here are some examples.

Vajraloka in North Wales is devoted to meditation. It holds retreats for men with an established meditation practice. Some of these are devoted to intensive engagement with the practice of mindfulness, the development of loving-kindness, or reflection, and some are for Order members only.
Taraloka, in Shropshire, England, is a retreat centre that is run by and for women. It holds some introductory retreats and its programme of events ranges from study seminars to intensive meditation retreats and retreats focusing on the arts.

Dharmavastu Buddhist Study Centre in North Wales is home to a resident community devoted to Dharma study. It runs seminars training Order members who teach at FWBO centres, and also more general study retreats.

Guhyaloka lies in a remote mountain valley in southern Spain. Each year two four-month ordination courses for men are held there. The valley is also home to a vihara – a community of men living a celibate life of meditation, reflection, and study.

Tiratanaloka, in beautiful South Wales countryside, is the base for retreats that help women prepare for ordination into the WBO. Like the men's equivalent, Padmaloka in Norfolk, it houses a community of senior members of the Order.

BUDDHAFIELD

In recent years a new way of operating has developed that does not fit into the pattern of FWBO centres and retreat centres. This began when some Order members started teaching meditation in a marquee at the Glastonbury Festival which (as well as being a huge rock festival) is the leading gathering for alternative lifestyles in the UK. Encouraged by the response, they started teaching at other festivals and

Above
View of the Spanish mountains from Guhyaloka Retreat Centre

Left
Dhanakosa Retreat Centre in Scotland

holding `camping retreats' on land near Glastonbury, and adopted the name `Buddhafield' for their work.

These events make Buddhist practice available to the thousands of people who identify with a subculture of British society, and might not visit a Buddhist centre. They are also a chance to be closer to nature, and to create a less institutional context than buildings can offer. 1997 saw the start of the Buddhafield Festival, which attracts up to fifteen hundred people each year. As well as activities led by people from the FWBO, it offers many activities led by people from other backgrounds and traditions.

REVIVING BUDDHISM IN INDIA

Buddhism was born in India, but 800 years ago it virtually died out in its birthplace. In the twentieth century it was spectacularly revived and there are now over 10,000,000 Indian Buddhists. The vast majority of these people are from communities whose members were considered `untouchables' under the Hindu caste system, and who became Buddhists as a result of a mass movement of conversion initiated in the 1950s.

TBMSG is one of the most prominent Buddhist movements in this community, and Indians are a significant part of the international community of the FWBO.

Caste and untouchability

The Hindu caste system – which has been described as a `system of graded inequality' – has divided India for thousands of years. According to this system, the level of society into which a person is born is their `fate' and individuals are powerless to change their social position. Those considered `untouchables' were beneath the caste system altogether, so inferior that caste Hindus considered that merely touching such a person would pollute them. Pushed to the fringes of society, they were denied religious and human rights, and forced to scrape a living from unpleasant and demeaning jobs.

At the time of the struggle for Indian independence, a brilliant lawyer called Dr Bhimrao Ambedkar emerged as the leader of this community. Dr Ambedkar was born into an `untouchable' community, but through extraordinary talent and hard work he rose to the top of the Indian legal profession. As architect of the Indian constitution, following independence in 1947, he framed the laws that banned the practice of untouchability.

Conversion to Buddhism

But (as the experience of American blacks following the abolition of slavery also showed) it is one thing to ban a form of oppression and quite another thing to overcome the attitudes that brought it into being, or its economic and psychological consequences.

Dr Ambedkar decided that the only way for the members of his community to be truly free was to leave Hinduism, and follow values that recognized the humanity of all, so that the community could transform itself. In 1956 he became a Buddhist, and in a mass-conversion ceremony he led several hundred thousand others into the new religion. But Dr Ambedkar died just six weeks after that ceremony, leaving the fledgling Buddhist movement in disarray. A young English bhikkhu with whom Ambedkar had discussed the conversion, named Sangharakshita, was one of those who helped the movement to survive. More conversions followed, but for many years little was done to put the spiritual principles these `new Buddhists' espoused into practice. Sangharakshita returned to Britain where he founded the FWBO, and in 1978 some of his disciples started teaching in India themselves. Activities started in Poona, in the western Indian state of Maharashtra. A new name was needed, so the Indian wing of the movement was called Trailokya Bauddha Mahasangha Sahayak Gana (TBMSG), which roughly translates as the Buddhist Fellowship of the entire Universe .

Activities quickly spread to other cities, and there are now twenty TBMSG centres

across India. Connected with these is the network of social work activities described earlier. Indians now comprise around one quarter of the Order, and the movement's activities in India involve many thousands of people.

Above
**Women's ordinations
in India**
photograph by
Devamitra

Left
**Learning to write
in India**
photograph by
Dhammarati, courtesy
of Karuna Trust

the FWBO at the millennium

At the time of writing, the FWBO is entering its thirty-fifth year and it has grown into a substantial, diverse, and complex movement. It faces numerous issues and challenges, so here is a snapshot of some of them.

The first issue is that of leadership after Sangharakshita. He has passed on his main responsibilities to a group of senior Order members based at Madhyamaloka in Birmingham. Central to this group are the three women and five men Public Preceptors, who are responsible for performing ordinations within the WBO, and it is with them that the future leadership of the movement principally lies. 2000 marked Sangharakshita's seventy-fifth birthday, and the date at which he passed on the headship of the Order to the College of Public Preceptors.

A second issue is size and diversification. The ever-increasing size of the Order means that the structures that ensure harmony and communication between its members need continually to be rethought and renewed if it is to continue as an effective spiritual community. This is a particular issue when there are cultural differences as great as those between members of the Ambedkarite community in India and Europeans or North Americans. Even in the West the FWBO has grown more diverse with the increasing range of ages and lifestyles of its members. New ways of thinking and working have to be developed to accommodate this.

At the same time, many people in the FWBO now have two or three decades of experience of committed Dharma practice, and situations are emerging that support greater depth and intensity. An example is the vihara at Guhyaloka in southern Spain. As Order members in the West gain their own deep-rooted experience of meditation and other forms of practice, new approaches and languages for practice are developing.

Above all, as the FWBO develops institutionally there is a concern that it maintains a challenging, experimental, and creative edge, and does not succumb to the dangers of institutionalization. It is committed to ensuring that its various manifestations are aids to practising the Dharma and Going for Refuge, rather than ends in themselves. But this can only be maintained by a constant renewal and reinvigoration.

A unified perspective

The FWBO's approach to the spiritual life might best be described as `holistic'. It is founded on the conviction that Buddhism has something of great value to offer people in the modern world and that this has implications for all aspects of life. That is why this introduction has looked at the FWBO from five perspectives. It is an approach to Buddhism, a spiritual community, an engagement with society, a path of practice, and a worldwide Buddhist movement. Looking at it from only one of these perspectives will give a partial understanding.

The picture that emerges is of a substantial and thriving Buddhist movement, which is attempting something difficult with a surprising degree of success. Looked at from one point of view the FWBO's approach to practising Buddhism in the modern world is radical – questioning old ways of living a Buddhist life and developing new forms for people in the modern world. Looked at in another way it is very traditional, emphasizing the key teachings that go back to the Buddha himself, and insisting on the spirit of devoted practice that alone gives them meaning. The FWBO is slowly finding a middle way that combines flexibility with fidelity to Buddhism's core values.

The arrival of Buddhism in the West is an extraordinary encounter in which the FWBO has a distinctive role. It cuts through much of the baffling diversity of the Buddhist tradition, and the cultural forms in which it has been embodied, to express the spirit that is at the heart of the tradition. As a spiritual community it offers a helpful emotional and social context for a spiritual life of devoted practice. The FWBO's social forms offer the opportunity for those who want them and can make use of them to live as full-time Buddhist practitioners in the heart of modern society. Its path of practice offers a systematic approach to training and transforming the mind in accordance with the Dharma. And as a worldwide Buddhist movement it is making the Buddha's teachings available to many people across the globe.

Of course, the FWBO is not without flaws. It is a community of individuals, each with his or her limitations, but its emphasis on Sangha gives people the chance to learn from each other and act together from their shared strengths, making a real difference to the world. It has much to offer the spiritual life of individuals, and a distinctive contribution to make to the Buddhist world.

The test of its approach is whether it offers a viable and effective way to follow the Buddhist path in the twenty-first century.

finding out more

Recommended Reading

INTRODUCTORY BUDDHISM

A Guide to the Buddhist Path
Sangharakshita

Human Enlightenment
Sangharakshita

Principles of Buddhism
Kulananda

Vision and Transformation
Sangharakshita

MEDITATION

Change Your Mind
Paramananda

Meditation: The Buddhist Way of Tranquillity and Insight
Kamalashila

WESTERN BUDDHISM AND THE FWBO

Buddhism and the West
Sangharakshita

Buddhism for Today and Tomorrow
Sangharakshita

Western Buddhism
Kulananda

SANGHARAKSHITA AND HIS TEACHING

A Survey of Buddhism
Sangharakshita

The Three Jewels
Sangharakshita

Sangharakshita: A New Voice in the Buddhist Tradition
Subhuti

Bringing Buddhism to the West: A Life of Urgyen Sangharakshita
Subhuti

FURTHER READING

A History of My Going of Refuge
Sangharakshita

Complete Poems 1941–1994
Sangharakshita

The Rainbow Road
Sangharakshita

Facing Mount Kanchenjunga
Sangharakshita

In the Sign of the Golden Wheel
Sangharakshita

RITUAL AND DEVOTION

Ritual and Devotion in Buddhism
Sangharakshita

Puja: The FWBO Book of Buddhist Devotional Texts

THE BUDDHIST REVIVAL IN INDIA

Ambedkar and Buddhism
Sangharakshita

Jai Bhim! Dispatches from a Peaceful Revolution
Terry Pilchick (Nagabodhi)

But Little Dust
Padmasuri

Magazines and Journals

Dharma Life
A magazine on the meeting of Buddhism and western culture
www.dharmalife.com

Lotus Realm
A magazine for women Buddhists

Urthona
A magazine of Buddhism and the arts

The Western Buddhist Review
Scholarship and reflection
www.westernbuddhistreview.com

Where to find us

There are 80 FWBO centres teaching meditation and Buddhism (plus many more groups) and FWBO activities in 24 countries. Here are some central contact addresses:

ENGLAND
London Buddhist Centre
51 Roman Road
London E2 0HU
Tel: 00 44 (20) 8981 1225
www.lbc.org.uk

SCOTLAND
Glasgow Buddhist Centre
329 Sauchiehall Street
Glasgow G2 3HW
Tel: 00 44 (141) 333 0524
www.glasgowbuddhistcentre.com

WALES
Cardiff Buddhist Centre
12 St Peter's Street
Cardiff CF24 3BA
Tel: 00 44 (29) 2046 2492

US: EAST COAST
Aryaloka Retreat Center
Heartwood Circle
Newmarket
NH 03857
Tel: 00 1 (603) 659 5456
www.aryaloka.org

US: WEST COAST
San Fransisco Buddhist Center
37 Bartlett Street
San Fransisco,
California CA94110
Tel: 00 1 (415) 282 2018
www.sfbuddhistcenter.org

AUSTRALIA
Sydney Buddhist Centre
24 Enmore Road
Newton
NSW 2042
Tel: 00 61 (2) 9519 0440
www.sydney.fwbo.org.au

BELGIUM
Buddhistisch Centrum Gent
Zebrastraat 37
9000 Gent
B9050
Tel: 00 32 (9) 231 2734

FINLAND
Helsingin Buddhalainen Keskus
Lonnrotinkatu 32 A 27
00180 Helsinki
Tel: 00 358 (9) 4368 3231
www.saunalahti.fi/fwbo

FRANCE
Centre Bouddhiste AOBO
25 Rue Concordet
Paris 75009
Tel: 00 33 (1) 4453 0731

GERMANY
Buddhistisches Zentrum Essen
Herkulesstrasse 13A
Essen 45127
Tel: 00 49 (201) 230155
www.fwbo.de

INDIA
TBMSG Poona
Dhammachakra Pravartana
Mahavihara
Raja Harishchandra Road
Dapodi, Poona 411012
Tel: 00 91 (212) 318174

IRELAND
Dublin Meditation Centre
2 East Essex Street
Temple Bar
Dublin 2
Tel: 00 353 (1) 671 3187

ITALY
Aobo Roma
Via Conca d'Oro 206
Int 33, scala B
Roma 00141
Tel: 00 39 (06) 8862 5565

MEXICO
Mexico City Buddhist Centre
Calle Juarez no 41
Col del Carmen Coyoacan
CP04100
Mexico City DF
Tel: 00 52 (5) 5659 8821
www.budismo.com

NETHERLANDS
Boeddhistisch Centrum Amsterdam
Palmstraat 63
1015 H P Amsterdam
Tel: 00 31 (20) 420 7097
www.vwbo.demon.nl

NEW ZEALAND
Auckland Buddhist Centre
PO Box 78-205
Grey Lynn
Auckland
Tel: 00 64 (9) 378 1120
mysite.xtra.co.nz/~auckbudcen

NORWAY
Oslo Buddhist Center
Disenveien 33
0587 Oslo
Tel: 00 47 (22) 22 33 44

SPAIN
Centro Budista de Valencia
Calle Literato Gabriel Miro, 5
Valencia 46008
Tel: 00 34 (96) 385 2596

SWEDEN
Vasterlandska Buddhistordens Vanner
Sodermannagaten 58, NB/OG
11665 Stockholm
Tel: 00 46 (8) 418 849
hem2.passagen.se/vbv

VENEZUELA
Centro Budista de Merida
Apartado 108
Merida 5101-a
Tel: 00 58 (74) 529602

There are also FWBO activities in Brazil, Canada, Denmark, Estonia, Greece, Russia, Singapore and South Africa.

FWBO WEBSITE
www.fwbo.org

ONLINE MEDITATION TEACHING
www.wildmind.org

KARUNA TRUST
St Mark's Studios
Chillingworth Road
London N7 8SJ
Tel: 00 44 (020) 7700 3434
www.karuna.org

WINDHORSE PUBLICATIONS
11 Park Road
Moseley, Birmingham
B13 8AB
Tel: 00 44 (121) 449 9191
www.windhorsepublications.com

CLEAR VISION
PRINTS, VIDEOS & EDUCATION
16-20 Turner Street
Manchester M4 1DZ
Tel: 00 44 (161) 839 9579
www.clear-vision.org

FWBO CENTRAL
Madhyamaloka
30 Chantry Road
Moseley
Birmingham B13 8DH
Tel: 00 44 (121) 449 3700

TARALOKA RETREAT CENTRE FOR WOMEN
Bettisfield
Whitchurch
Shropshire SY13 2LD
Tel: 00 44 (1948) 710 646
www.taraloka.org.uk

RIVENDELL RETREAT CENTRE
Chillies Lane
High Hurstwood
East Sussex TN22 4AB
Tel: 00 44 (1825) 732 594

DHANAKOSA RETREAT CENTRE
Ledcreich House
Balquhidder
Lochearnhead
Perthshire FK19 8PQ
Scotland
Tel: 00 44 (1877) 384 213
www.dhanakosa.com

BUDDHAFIELD
TRAVELLING FWBO
PO Box 27822
London SE24 9YZ
Tel: 00 44 (7768) 200 797
www.buddhafield.com